# Inspiring Thoughts

Irfan Alam

ISBN 978-93-5610-735-9

Published in India 2022 by Pencil

**Contributors:**
Editor: Priya

*A brand of*
One Point Six Technologies Pvt. Ltd.
123, Building J2, Shram Seva Premises,
Wadala Truck Terminal, Wadala (E)
Mumbai 400037, Maharashtra, INDIA
**E** connect@thepencilapp.com
**W** www.thepencilapp.com

DISCLAIMER: *The opinions expressed in this book are those of the authors and do not purport to reflect the views of the Publisher.*

# Author biography

Irfan Alam hails from the valley of Jammu and Kashmir, India. Completed his Post Graduation in English Literature, poetry fascinated him right from the very childhood and manifested the dynamic side of his life. The flavours of poetry influenced him in a fantastic way and uses it as a tool of great meaningful expression of ideas and thoughts.

# CONTENTS

# Foreword

Love is to bear all the pain
as the mother to give a new birth,
How could it be different for love
which gives birth to a new Self.

These inspiring thoughts, emotions and outbursts of great expressions makes us delve deep into the ocean to think about the world around us. These quotes in the form of a book makes us converse with ourselves and reflect upon the divine aspect that is already embedded in us and all we need is to realise this potential and transcend this human self.

These thoughts and insights colours life with different hues and make the reader have a look at it and draw something new. There are many divine aspects also that want us to converse with God and see through the divine light where all the darkness fades away and we see the truth with our naked eye. This divine light that ignites our imner self makes us godly and divine, all we need is to polish the mirror of this heart and it will reflect the light of God. So, these intuitional and deep emotions renderings make us dive deep into the ocean and find richest of pearls.

# Preface

It was Autumn
I buried the seeds
of sorrow into my garden
And spring came
They grew into beautiful flowers
And now people ask me
to give us the seeds of the flowers.

These deep renderings, great emotions and intuitional insights in the form of book entitled "Inspiring Thoughts" is an attempt to portray life in its different shades and colours. As we see this life is a beautiful lie and we have to accept and live by that lie.

So, the book gives us great lessons about life and its real meaning and brings us very close to God to see through the divine light thus taking us away from the darkness.

# Acknowledgements

In writing this book I am greatly thankful to my parents, especially my wife, and all my friends who put all their efforts to support me and showed great patience at every stage.

I am also thankful to Pencil Publishers who made this book available to the general reader which infact would have been a task impossible.

# Prologue

It was the Autumn
I buried the seeds
of sorrow into my garden
And the Spring came
they grew into beautiful flowers.
Now, people ask me
to give us the seeds of the flowers.

This life is a play
and we the players.
Each of us plays the role
and finally leaves the stage
and is heard no more.

Sometimes the soul dances within
sometimes the flame
grows higher.
At another times
we are many beings
in one being
because of love.

We are the shining pearls
gleaming all so bright
in the darkness of the night.
Why cover it
with the cloak
of greed and lust
and hide its lustre.

Looking at the mirror
I saw this image
of Me within me.
And polishing the mirror
this Me became We
that made the only difference.

Take the path
the way will appear.
Staying back home
we will never reach the destiny.

Life is like a rainbow
you see in it
beautiful colours
is actually a mere show
of colours and nothing else.

Is it fair to love someone
at the cost of thy life
and know that this life
is nothing but an illusion!

I walked in the street
to see a perfect man.
And people just laughed at me
Ridiculing ---- Saying a mad person
But I knew all what they meant
and what I

You're a nightingale
to sing the songs most divine.
Why are you acting
like an ominous bird?

Through all my life
I have been silent
and now silence sings
the song of my heart.

Enter the garden
take the fragrance
of the rose bed.
Why are you counting
the thorns there?

This cup of wine is life
let me drink it
to the full brim
and know the meaning
of love and its intoxication.

Who is calling me -----
A strange voice.
When I looked back
it was no one,
So, I searched and searched
and found it no where
but within the Self.

Open the door
see through the inner eye
don't close it -----
There is a mine of gold inside
that rarely we see
through a naked eye.

Come, I am saying two things.
Remember.
One, you never let lose the rein
of your horse either he will
become the master.
Two, tame this animal
so as to be its master.

You are worth pure gold
that needs to be purified -----
This love is the alchemy
that transcends everything
but needs a little labour.

I am a torren cloth
that needs to be sewed
by the master tailor
to give it a final shape.
Either it will go waste
to be thrown away.

Remember, this body is a prison house.
To escape from it
and break those chains
you've to hear the advice of this SELF.

Wait, be patient, think -----
Speak less, at times be silent.
These qualities are so rare
that transforms a person.

This soul and mind
are two different entities.
One speaks the language of Love
and another, to experience things,
Can both be measured
in the same balance?

Close this door of empty world
this mere show of delusion
let you open the door
of the real existence
where soul meets the soul.

See the light, walk, Walk through -----
You may stumble, Stand;
At every fall you'll learn a new thing
that it was my fault
but each time you stand
you'll never be the same.

You're a beautiful flower
whose fragrance is so delightful.
Don't make it look sick and ugly
by the Autumn breeze.

I was dancing in frenzy and madness
whirling like a dervish,
As love made me to drink with the cup
pouring it to the full brim.

O traveller of the night!
Where are you going
without a guide?
Though the stars are gleaming bright
but still you find no destiny.

This life has taught me strange things
but still I don't know
the meaning of my nothingness.

You who are seeking Love
and yearning for it
go little mad and crazy enough
burn like a candle
the path is full of hurdles.
Go through.
Definitely, you'll reach destiny.

Arise, time will reveal you
at the right time.

I was searching for love
and yearning for it
to find that true serenity
but this darkness of my heart
made it look so pity a sight.

This whole creation is just
as the whirling dance of a dervish
and God the mover.

This silence speaks a language
but needs a heart
to sing its tune.

Love is to bear all the pain
as the mother to give a new birth.
How could it be different for Love
that gives birth to a new Self.

Self is resplendent with divine light
to hide it is to conceal things
but how the radiance of the Sun
can be concealed when it rises.

We are in between
belief and disbelief.
Move ahead there is a field
other than this.

We doubt about things
knowing very little
the answer lies within
but we never realise
this great hidden power.

The Sun sets,
the Moon disappears.
But how long their truth
will remain hidden.

Attachment to this world temporary
make us suffer and tarnish.
While attaching this Self
towards the love of God
makes us the real being.

Listen the deep calling
of your heart
there is an Ocean inside
dive deep into it
and find the rare pearl.

This Love is a four letter word
but heals the whole world
and wins everyone.

The path is full of thorns
with many entanglements
let's be patient as roses
to give the sweet fragrance.

Realise yourself
and you will know the secrets
of hidden mysteries.

Another day,
Yet another occasion
I meet this life
and say welcome
to have you
but sad not knowing it.

The positive thing is that
you are what you are
and the negative element
not knowing what you are.

We must dream
but the real thing is to fulfill
and make it into a reality.

Each day is your new start
each and every moment yours only
Yesterday is past,
Tomorrow is decisive,
Live by this word Now.

The big tragedy is not death
but living life
as dying each moment inside
without knocking the door of reality.

Throw out this worldly garment of no value
inside you there is a hidden treasure
find the ruby and get the applause
living with kings and princes.

True freedom is when body breaks
all the ties with these wishes
and desires of world temporary
and soul meeting the soul.

Love springs from the fountain
of purity and its real essence
is to purify things and join hearts.

Talking no matter how sweet
and humble-seeming its music may be
let silence be the art we practice.

The tavern is open
and saki is pouring the wine
hold the cup, be drunk in this love
forgetting everything mudane.

It is better to slip, fall down and get up
than the one who sits
and watches how one falls,
laughing.

Break this I
and tore it into pieces
let it be joined with the great bond
of Divine Love.

I am bankrupted by my own desires
and now I try to repair this loss
through the great treasure of Love inside.

We weep or shed tears
only to release our pain.
But the eyes of true lovers
shed them for joy and ecstasy.

O impudent one!
You're after this pageant show
and like a child you are dazzled by it
finding it reality not knowing the actuality
that it is a childish play.

Contentment is true wisdom
as you pour out the sea into a pitcher
how much will it hold.

You're an Ocean inside
and its water, the flow of Love.

The Sun rises to embrace the day,
the moon brightens to embrace the night
that is how things exactly go in contrast
but stay there and wait.

You obey your mind
and dig holes for others
and in the long run
you're caught in your own trap
but there is no escape.

You're what you are
don't imitate or copy things.
What things are, are, What not, not ----
You are the true image of yourself
others a mere show.

Once I threw a pebble into the river
and countless ripples there
touched the surface
but when it reached the depth
it became still.

Living life without purpose
is a journey of no destination.
So give your whole self
to find that true purpose.

O haughty one!
You're engaged to the wedlock
of this temporary world.
Untie this knot and tie it
to the everlasting bond of Love and Friendship.

In this life I acted
everytime as a villian
and never knew
that there was a real hero
inside me to get the applause.

The candle is burning
with the flame growing higher
let my love be its part
and burn into ashes
till I say to Self how did you like it.

Past is a way you already have left
and present is the wagon
in which you ride towards the future.

Death reveals us in many ways
We are ignorant of this fact.
As the Sun sets, the moon disappears
but actually this setting and disappearing
is a new beginning.

Death you fear is nothing
but the beginning of another world
Where eyes see the true reality of things.

How the colours of life change
but still we don't accept them
as we never choose the perfect colours.

There may come many hurdles,
A howling storm or another chaos
but never lose hope, trust, trust God
He will save you as Joseph from the well.

Who I am
I am
What I am
I am not.
Yet this being
and not being
has a meaning.

Reason always argues
how things should look
reaching nowhere
While love knows everything
but remains silent, all so silent.

Set a goal, move along
through and through.
Finding shortcuts
we will never reach the destination.

Myself I think what is this life
but a mere show of delusion.
We play this show
and then see it no more.

You is the strength,
You the power.
Let this You find you.

We are all the episodes
of these dancing flames
of the candle ----
Dancing, dancing and dancing
Untill we burn in this Love.

Catch this Now,
Why are you thinking of tomorrow.
Yet tomorrow comes
still you don't catch this Now.

Me asked a question to me
in reply I asked me to be silent,
silent, so silent
as the Ocean.

All this love and yearning
for the beloved is an endless journey
to take us to our real existence.

Your ship may be tossed
by the great storm,
Don't lose hope ----
When you've faith and trust upon God
then you will be saved as Younis
from the darkness of the whale.

I fell prey to these desires
and never thought of the power
of this Self
that made the only difference
between my animality and being human.

I shredded my outer garment
in the rapture of the beloved
now I try to sew it with this divine love.

The epitome of this life
is to stay, strive, struggle
and never lose hope.

Stand before you fall,
Win before you lose,
Succeed before you fail ----
Every step you take
is the attempt towards progress.
Never say never.

Play this game called life
to the end,
Don't say I am tired
Never lose hope.
Definitely every step that you take
will lead you to success.

Yesterday is past,
Tomorrow is yours only,
And don't worry about the future,
It is yet to come.

All these sins and this falling prey
to my desires and body becoming slave
to this material world
has turned Mana into Gall
and this fertile land into a ruined desert.

Things happen and things go
that is how the routine of this life goes
But how many times do we think
how things are.

The moment I am with my beloved
Everything else seems a dream
and mere illusion.

We give priority to these vain desires
and rely on this false appearance
thus losing the most precious entity
Soul, the most divine.

What is the meaning of this life
when the soul is wandering in great void
not knowing its true essence
then animals are better than we humans.

I was bleeding inside
and the doors closed too
but when I opened the window of this love
I saw the garden full of roses and flowers.

Divine are these inner voices
deep the meaning of the reality of this life
but when do we hear these voices
and deep meaning of life.

I turned this wheel of fate all my life
and broke those spokes
in the middle of the path
Now, I bind them to love knot
and find only love.

All this loneliness and pain kills me inside

but one mention of the name of my beloved
all this pain and loneliness vanish from this heart.

Polish this heart with divine love
and see the mirror reflects it in the same way.

I stole my bread from a false plate
and never tried to earn it from the true one.

Desires make us a slave to our body
To control it let us hear the voice
of divine soul inside.

This yearning and all this burning
is love and of love
and I love being crazy and mad in this love.

I entered the garden to console my anguish
but the season of the Autumn
has left it more desolate
but when I opened the gate of this love
I felt ashamed as there I found no season at all
but only love.

Those who are seeking love
go little crazy and mad enough
as moth jumps into the flame
knowing no consequences
all it wants is to get love.

You knock the door but it doesn't open
as you follow the reason
but when you open the love door
all the secrets are revealed so clear
as it hears the voice of heart.

This love has taught me one thing
that love can be understood
by the language of love.

You are a falcon to take flight
above the sky all so free
why are you caged in this earthly prison.

The demons haunt us when evil spreads
and that is the real death of mankind
and to cast out these demons
Let goodness prevail through love.

Bravery is not to defeat anyone
in the battle field
but the real courage and bravery
is to hold anger when it matters.

Listen to the call of your heart
just stay there, every beating you hear
gives the message Love, Love, Love ----

Don't go to the river
where there is no thirst at all
for love of the beloved.

To expect from others
we reach no way near the destination
to reach the summit let this You find you.

So many secrets are hidden behind the veil
and let these secrets be revealed
one by one.

When we love each other
we forget distances
the only thing that matters is
how much we love.

We grope in darkness and fall down
but we never try to ignite
this divine light inside to shine things.

Think, think big, Love,
love with open heart, Share,
share with all, happiness and love.
In the end, you'll meet what you thought,
loved and shared.

True freedom is when the body breaks
all the ties with these wishes and desires
of the world temporary
and soul meeting the soul.

Love springs from the fountain of purity
and its true essence is to purify things
and join hearts.

Ah, many a times I think in my mind
to forsake things and forget everything
but each time heart makes a compromise.

How long will we be enchanted
by this false show.
Let the self wake up
and find the truth of being.

Don't tell me who I am
but what I am.

I let things go from my side
and never thought about the return
but yet I knew the things I let go
will not go in waste.

I expected things from others
in this hope of expectation
I lost everything that was mine.

I opened the door of this love
and saw flowers blooming there everytime
without the season of the Autumn.

I always let things go on my way
and never the way they go.

You're the hope of tomorrow
and today belongs always to you.

Things are temporary as is this world
but it is the good deeds that are
permanent, accountable and accomplishing.

I once threw a stone at Majnoon
in my childhood
not knowing the power of love.

I made my mind to think and doubt things
but heart made me to love
the truth of them inside.

Expecting from others everything
is to have nothing
and believing in yourself
is to have everything.

Love is a madman,
Working his wild schemes,
Dancing crazy, tearing clothes,
drinking poison,
and quietly choosing annihilation.

Speak to soul with silence,
Silence reveals more than language.

Hundreds of voices go against
but realise there is at least something
that you expect is in real favour of you.
Believe in that truth.

Sit with lovers and you'll learn new things,
Choose their state with this heart open,
Speechless and absolutely silent.

We're evolving each and every next day
but each time we are blinded
by our ignorance to know the truth.

Silence is the language of heart
its beauty lies in to remain silent,
Don't make it look ugly through wild talk.

We are all prisoners in this material world
shackled in the chains of desire and lust.
The only way to break these shackles
is to tame this Great Self.

www.ingramcontent.com/pod-product-compliance
Lightning Source LLC
LaVergne TN
LVHW050412160726
843469LV00041B/1042

* 9 7 8 9 3 5 6 1 0 7 3 5 9 *